Called to His Purpose

An Adult Coloring Book for Women

Vol. 2

Shawn R. McLeod

Called To His Purpose:
An Adult Coloring Book for Women
Vol. 2
By Shawn R. McLeod

And we know that all things work together for good to them that love God, to them who are the called according to his purpose.
—Romans 8:28

Copyright © 2019 Shawn R. McLeod - Living Your Purpose, LLC

Website: www.LYPurpose.org
Email: shawn@lypurpose.org

Graphic & Cover Design: Breyana Henderson| bstylegraphics@gmail.com
Editor: Shanda Brown | slanaybrown@gmail.com

All rights reserved.
No part of this publication may be reproduced, stored in a retrieval system or transmitted by any form or by any means electronic, recording or otherwise without the prior permission in writing from the publisher.

Unauthorized reproduction of any part of this publication by any means, including photocopying is an infringement of copyright.
ISBN# 978-0-9827035-3-3

Color to Clarify the Vision & Create the Reality

The Living Your Purpose Vision:

To teach women the principles of harnessing their imagination for kingdom manifestation.

Why Color?

- Lose yourself in the activity, relax your brain
- Obtain the reward for completing your own personal work of art
- Gather insight, use imagination and tap into your creativity

Instructions:

- Read text on the coloring page
- Meditate on the scriptures
- Begin coloring while reflecting on God's Word
- Sing songs to the Lord as you color
- Respond to the scriptures and writing prompts on each page
- Fill the lines with writing what God is showing you
- See yourself growing and soaring

Supplies:

- Your favorite coloring instruments, such as colored pencils, crayons, and markers.

> *Gather a strategic team of godly-smart individuals as advisors to achieving your vision.*
> *Don't try to do it all yourself.*

> God is your water source. Staying connected to him causes you to bear the Fruit of purpose.

*Worry is a distraction.
Shake it off with prayer, praise and worship.*

> *A seed must bear the pressure
> of being buried and broken, to be able to bud
> and finally spring forth.*

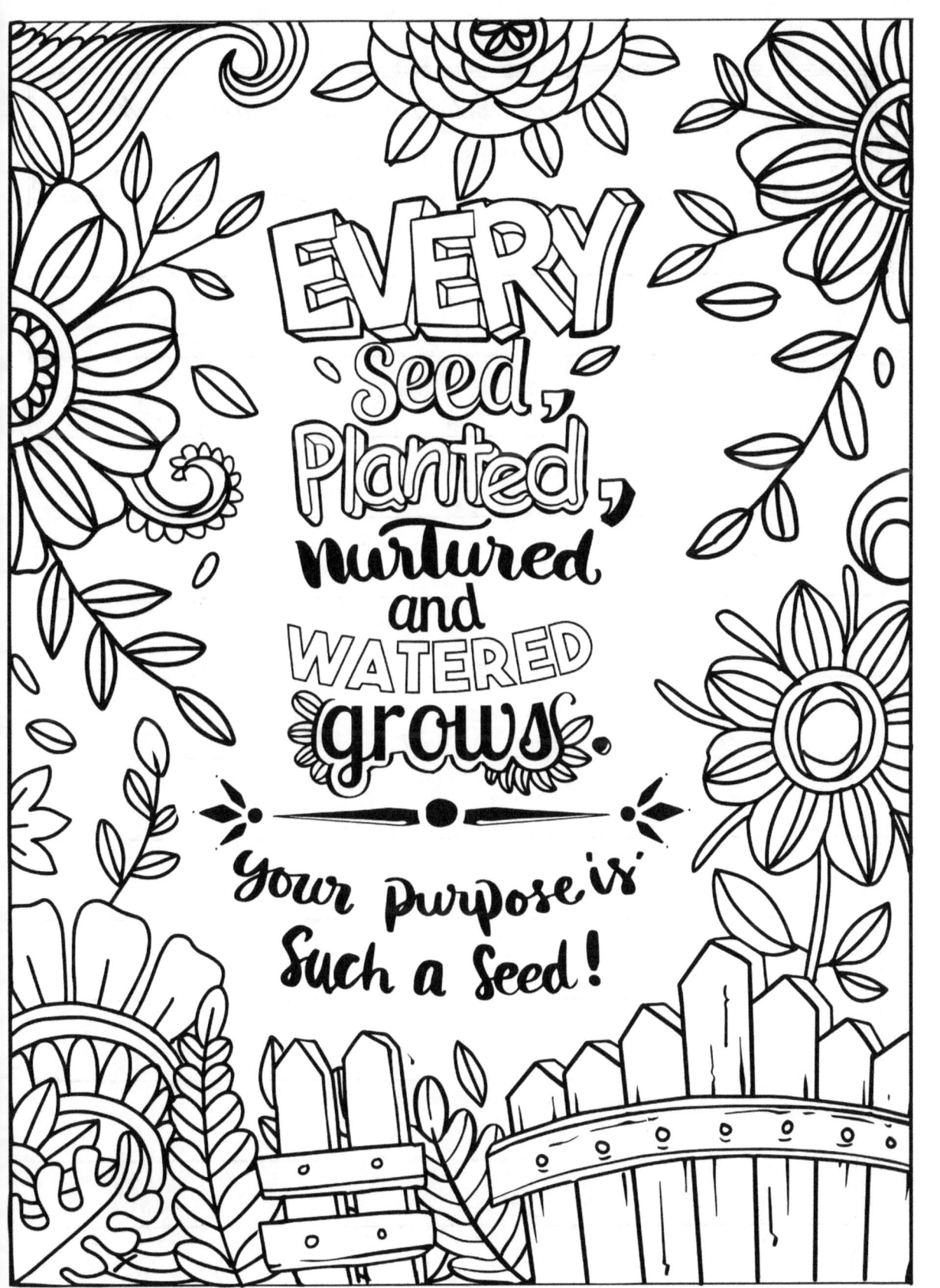

> *My Father's Strong pavilion is a sanctuary, shelter, and a fortress for my soul.*

> *Even during the most difficult times in your life you can be sure that you will get through it! He will be with you.*

WHEN YOU WALK THROUGH THE WATERS

I WILL BE WITH YOU

and through

The Rivers

They Will Not Overflow You.

Isaiah 43:2

> *It's so easy for other things to take God's place on the throne of your heart. Don't let it. Your Lord is calling you into His service.*

Forgive without delay!
It's healing to Your soul.

I need His mercy every day of my life!

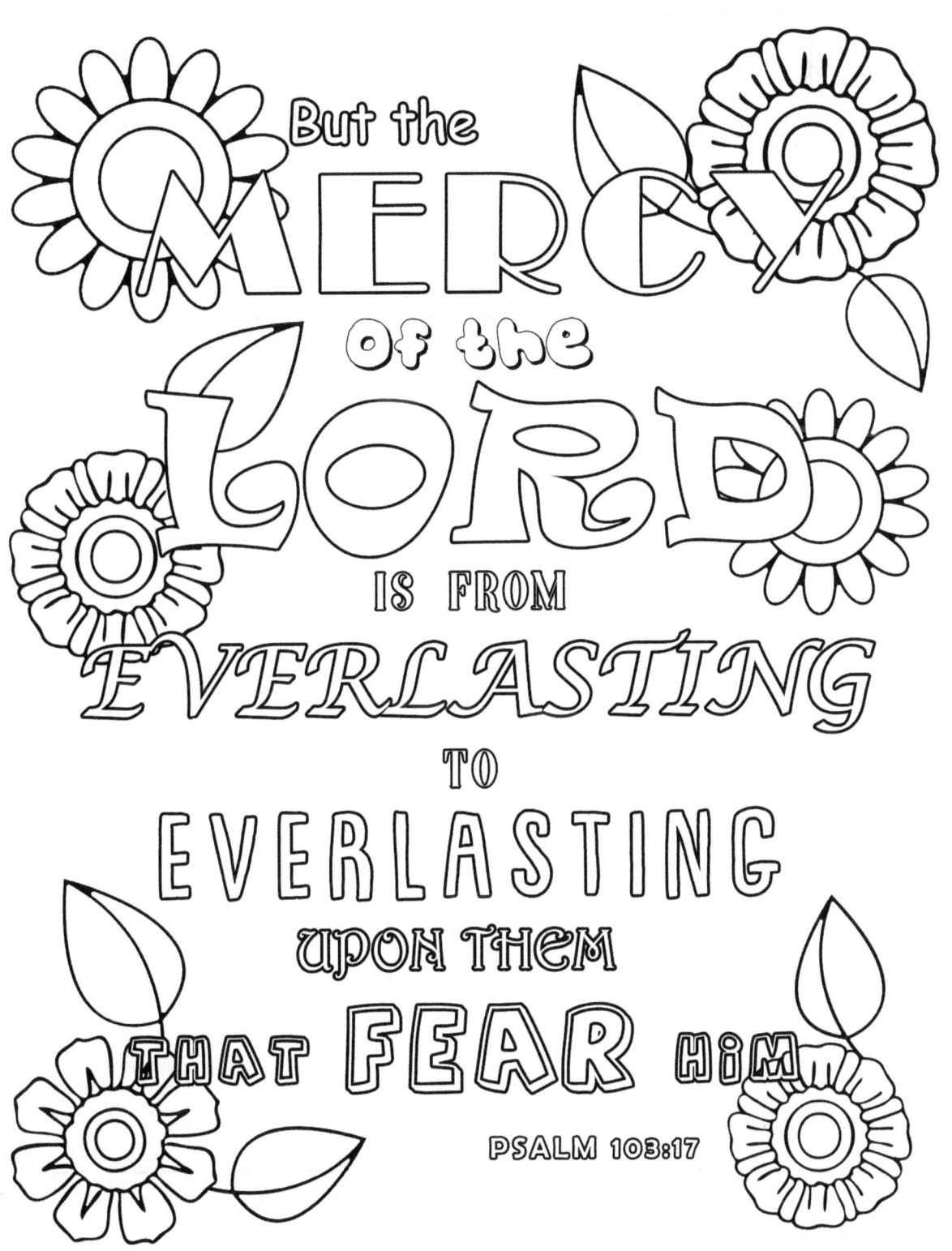

> *The Lord has already gone ahead of you.*
> *Take possession of your inheritance.*

Take possession

> The land you are crossing the Jordan to take possession of is a land of mountains and valleys that drink rain from heaven. - Deut. 11:11

> Only as a result of the work of the Holy Spirit in our lives can we exhibit His wonderful personality.

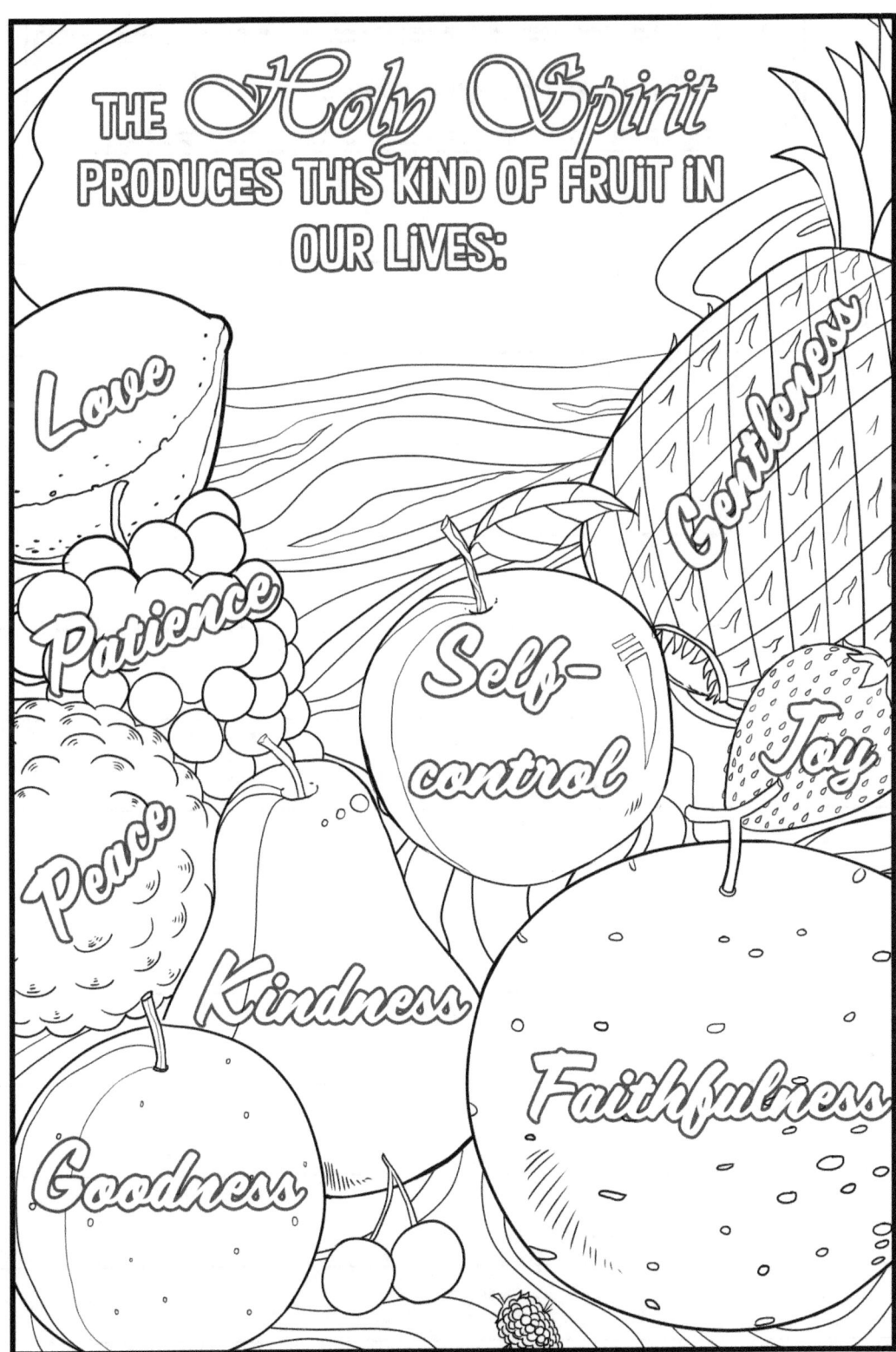

He is daily perfecting you in Him.

> *The Lord by his Spirit will give you the words to speak. You're His vessel delivering His Words in the right time, bringing relief and encouragement.*

> *Present yourself to the Lord daily for His use, for accomplishing His purpose, assignment by assignment.*

> *The Word of God will help you to guard your heart in spite of disappointment, tragedy, betrayal, and setbacks.*

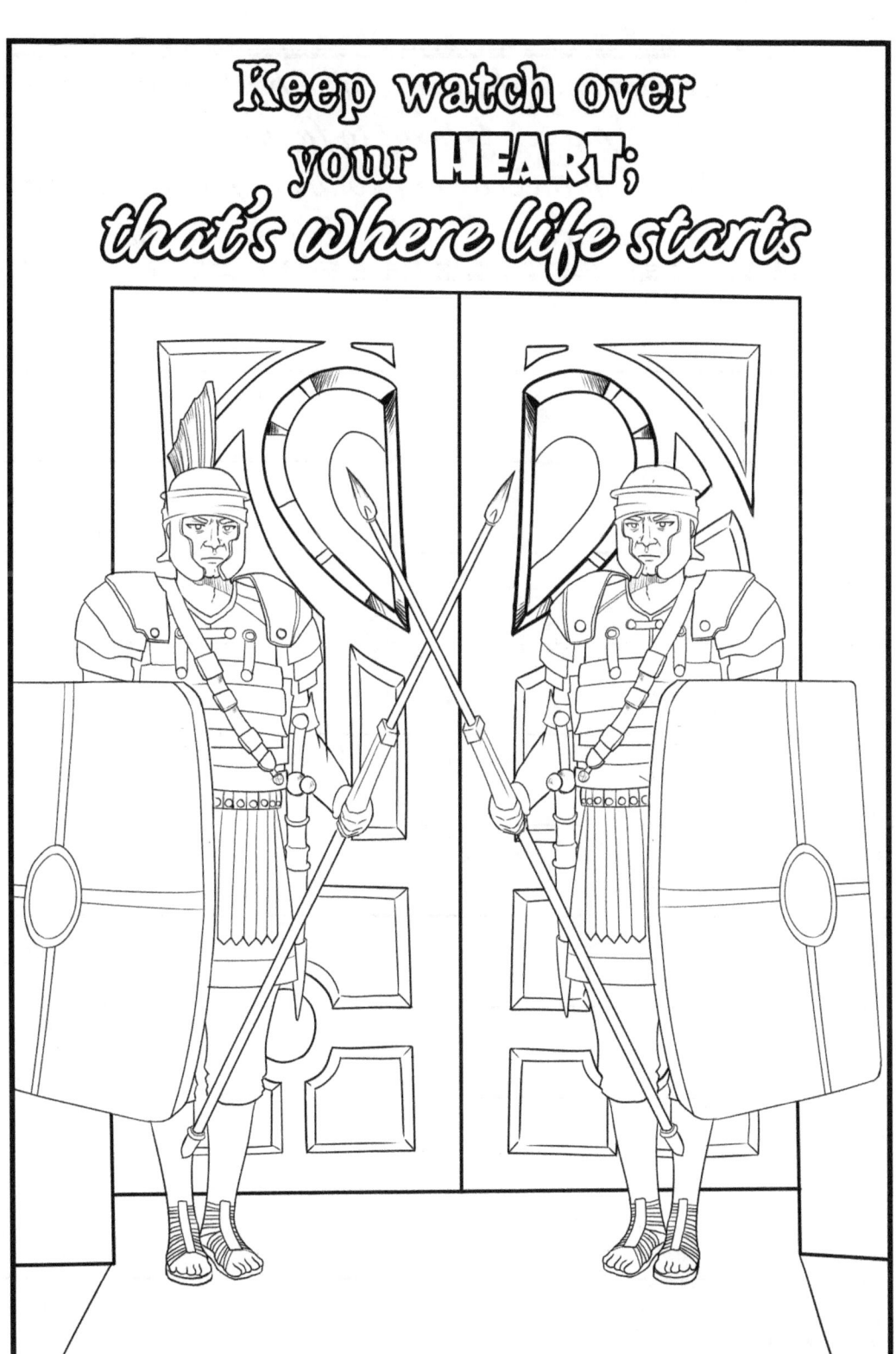

> *You can't see the end. Life's path looks like a maze, difficult to figure out.*
> *But, with the Lord in control, you know He will accomplish his purpose in you.*

> *Go ahead...imagine it. If you allow Him,*
> *He can do it through you.*

> *Even when we can't see it, God is at work.*
> *Keep walking forward.*

> *The Lord will keep and strengthen you as you walk through your wilderness.*

> *It will take everything you've got to resist the world's mold.*
> *How? Rebuild and renew your mind with God's word.*

> When it looks as if you are outnumbered, know He is right by your side, fighting on your behalf. He always wins.

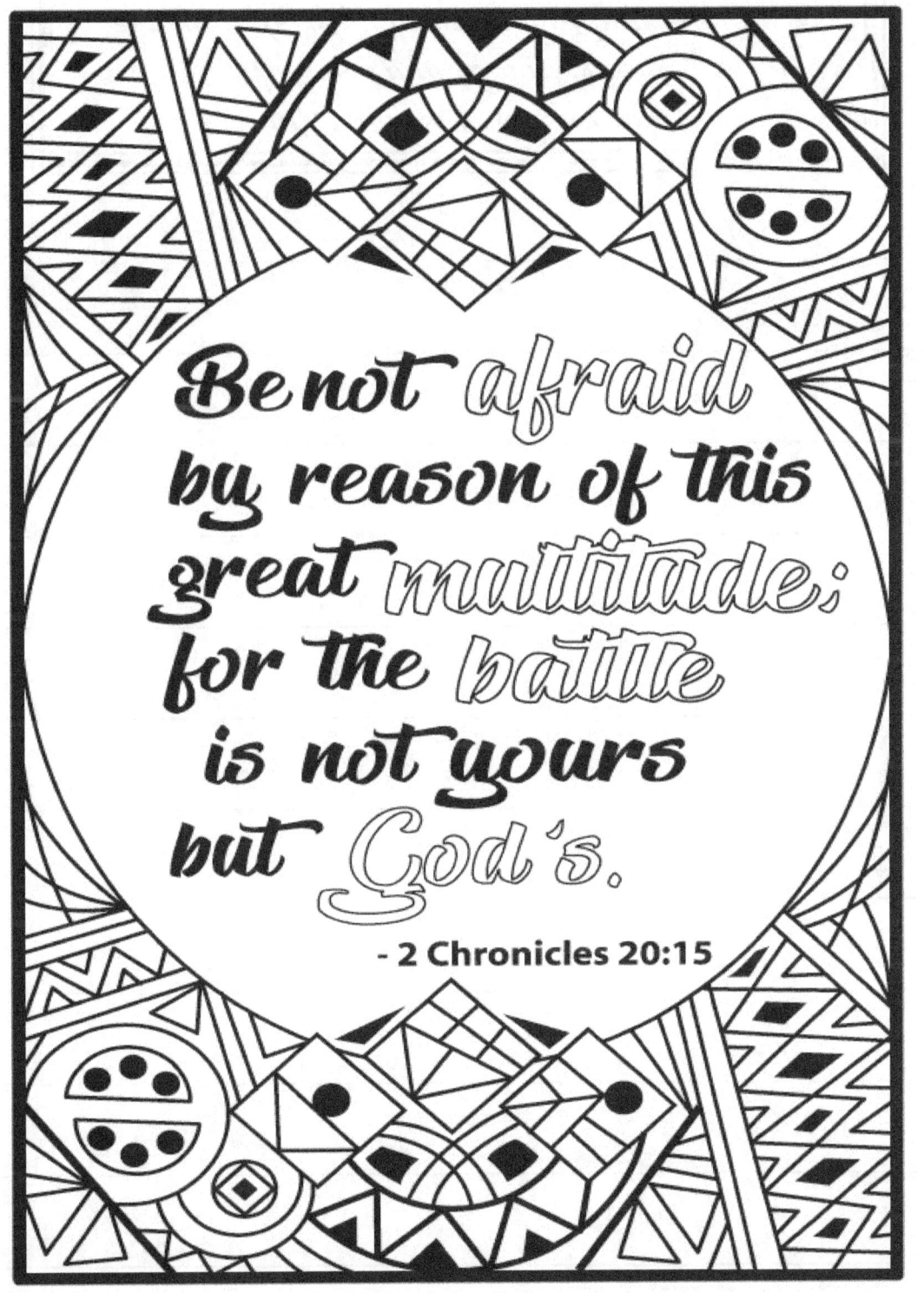

> *It's in the daily connection of prayer, praise,
> thanksgiving, and worship
> that we get closer to Him.*

> *Going after Your Lord does take intention and dedication.*

> You have a Heavenly Father who thinks of you constantly. He has your answers before you even call. Our Lord anticipates perfectly. It's called omniscience. Call to Him.

> *You can't bear His kind of fruit unless you are joined with Him.*

Buy with no money, all your needs met in Him!

See things from His perspective.

Seek those things which are above.

(Colossians 3:1)

www.ingramcontent.com/pod-product-compliance
Lightning Source LLC
Chambersburg PA
CBHW060520300426
44112CB00017B/2735